Try Not To Laugh Challenge

Challenge

Camping Trip Edition Joke Book

How To Play

Step 1

Split into two teams whether that be boys vs girls, kids vs parents, or any mix of your choice. If possible, also assign one person as a referee. You can also do 1 vs 1!

Step 2

Decide who gets to go first. Which team can do the most pushups? Which team can guess the number between 1 and 10 from someone not playing the game? Or just a good old fashioned rock paper scissors?

Step 3

The starting team has to tell a joke from the book. You can say the joke however you like and animate it too with funny faces, gestures, or whatever else.

Step 4

If everyone on the opposing team laughs, the other team gets a point! Set a limit for how many points it takes to win and the first team to reach the limit, wins!

What do you call a magic dog?

A Labracadabrador

What do you call a dinosaur that crashes his car?

Tyrannosaurus wrecks!

What do sharks say when something cool happens?

Jawesome

What do you call a pile of cats?

A meow-tain

What did one egg say to the other?

You're cracking me up!

What kind of nut has no shell?

A doughnut

How did the egg get up the mountain?

It scrambled up!

What do you give a sick lemon?

Lemon-aid

What do you call a dear with no eyes?

(In a southern accent) I have no idear!

How does a pirate prefer to travel?

By ARRRRRR-V

What did the beaver say to the tree?

Been nice gnawing you!

What kind of tree can fit in your hand?

A palm tree

Why don't lobsters share?

They're shellfish.

What did the big tree say to the little tree?

Leaf me alone!

What do you get when you cross a dinosaur with fireworks?

Dinomite

How do trees get on the internet?

They log in.

What did the tree do when the bank closed?

It opened another branch!

What did Oh Henry say when he saw the Hot Tamale?

Hubba Bubba

What do you say to a one legged hitch hiker?

Hop in!

Why did the duck say bang?

Because he was a firequacker!

What did the doughnut go to the dentist for?

To get a chocolate filling.

Why did the Oreo go to the dentist?

Because it lost its filling!

Why did the M&M go to college?

Because he wanted to be a Smarty!

What's tree plus tree?

Sticks

Why was the baker so angry?

He woke up on the wrong side of the bread!

What did the loaf of bread say to the angry man?

Rye so serious?

What's a dad's favorite treat?

POPsicles

What kind of shirts do Dads like to wear when golfing?

Tee shirts

What's a dad's favorite snack?

POPcorn

Why did Dad want to go fishing?

He was hooked on it!

What do you call a wolf that uses bad language?

A swearwolf

Who are the werewolf's cousins?

What-wolf and when-wolf

What time do ducks wake up?

At the quack of dawn!

What kind of vegetables are angry?

Steamed vegetables

Why did you invite the mushroom to the party?

Cause he's a fun-gi!

My sibling and I had an argument today...

It was in-tents!

Want to hear a campfire joke?

It's straight fire.

What do camping and fancy hotels have in common?

Toilet trees are complementary.

If you enjoyed this title, check out our other books by searching "Hayden Fox" on Amazon!

Printed in Germany
by Amazon Distribution
GmbH, Leipzig

16377289R00064